KOKOMO SCHOOL BOOKSTORE RENTAL BOOK

1. This book is not to be bought or sold.
2. Do not use this book to carry loose paper, notebooks, or pencils.
3. Do not mark in this book, or mutilate it in any way.
4. If this book is lost or damaged, the one renting it will be held responsible.
5. No book will be rented for a longer time than one school year.
6. Pupils moving from the city or withdrawing from school must return all rental books before leaving.
7. Pupils failing to return any rental book will be denied the right to rent books in the future.

TREASURY OF LITERATURE

Color the Sky

SENIOR AUTHORS
ROGER C. FARR
DOROTHY S. STRICKLAND

AUTHORS
RICHARD F. ABRAHAMSON
ELLEN BOOTH CHURCH
BARBARA BOWEN COULTER
BERNICE E. CULLINAN
MARGARET A. GALLEGO
W. DORSEY HAMMOND
JUDITH L. IRVIN
KAREN KUTIPER
DONNA M. OGLE
TIMOTHY SHANAHAN
PATRICIA SMITH
JUNKO YOKOTA
HALLIE KAY YOPP

SENIOR CONSULTANTS
ASA G. HILLIARD III
JUDY M. WALLIS

CONSULTANTS
ALONZO A. CRIM
ROLANDO R. HINOJOSA-SMITH
LEE BENNETT HOPKINS
ROBERT J. STERNBERG

HARCOURT BRACE & COMPANY
Orlando Atlanta Austin Boston San Francisco Chicago Dallas New York
Toronto London

Acknowledgments

For permission to reprint copyrighted material, grateful acknowledgment is made to the following sources:

Clarion Books, a Houghton Mifflin Company imprint: Five Little Monkeys Jumping on the Bed by Eileen Christelow. Copyright © 1989 by Eileen Christelow.

Ell-Bern Publishing Company (ASCAP): "You'll Sing a Song and I'll Sing a Song," lyrics and music by Ella Jenkins. Lyrics and music copyright © 1966, assigned 1968 to Ella Jenkins.

Greenwillow Books, a division of William Morrow & Company, Inc.: My Best Friend by Pat Hutchins. Copyright © 1993 by Pat Hutchins.

Harcourt Brace & Company: Cover illustration from *The Cow That Went OINK* by Bernard Most. Copyright © 1990 by Bernard Most.

HarperCollins Publishers: "Very Tall Mouse and Very Short Mouse" from *Mouse Tales* by Arnold Lobel. Copyright © 1972 by Arnold Lobel. From *Some Things Go Together* by Charlotte Zolotow. Text copyright © 1969 by Charlotte Zolotow.

Little, Brown and Company (Inc.): Cover illustration by Giles Laroche from *Sing a Song of People* by Lois Lenski. Illustration copyright © 1987 by Giles Laroche.

Lothrop, Lee & Shepard Books, a division of William Morrow & Company, Inc.: How Joe the Bear and Sam the Mouse Got Together by Beatrice Schenk de Regniers, illustrated by Bernice Myers. Text copyright © 1965 by Beatrice Schenk de Regniers; illustrations copyright © 1990 by Bernice Myers.

Orchard Books, New York: Cover illustration by James E. Ransome from *Do Like Kyla* by Angela Johnson. Illustration copyright © 1990 by James E. Ransome. *Together* by George Ella Lyon, illustrated by Vera Rosenberry. Text copyright © 1989 by George Ella Lyon; illustrations copyright © 1989 by Vera Rosenberry.

Philomel Books, a division of The Putnam & Grosset Group: Cover illustration by Masayuki Yabuuchi from *Animal Mothers* by Atsushi Komori. Illustration copyright © 1977 by Masayuki Yabuuchi. Originally published in Japan by Fukuinkan Shoten, Publishers, Ltd., 1977. *Whose Baby?* by Masayuki Yabuuchi. Copyright © 1981 by Masayuki Yabuuchi.

Random House, Inc.: Cover illustration by Lynn Munsinger from *My New Boy* by Joan Phillips. Illustration copyright © 1986 by Lynn Munsinger.

Marian Reiner, on behalf of Lilian Moore: "Friend" from *Little Raccoon and Poems from the Woods* by Lilian Moore. Text copyright © 1975 by Lilian Moore.

Illustration Credits

Key: (t) top, (b) bottom, (c) center.

Table of Contents Art
Thomas Vroman Associates, Inc., 4, 5

Bookshelf Art
Thomas Vroman Associates, Inc., 6, 7

Theme Opening Art
John Jones 8, 9; Anni Matsick, 92, 93

Selection Art
Vera Rosenberry, 10–37; Jackie Snider, 38–39; Eileen Christelow, 40–64; Masayuki Yabuuchi, 66–91; Bernice Myers, 108–136; Lilian Moore, 137; Arnold Lobel, 138–144

Dear Reader,

A good way to meet new people and go to new places is right in your hands. The pages of this book will let you meet many new characters and will take you to new places. You'll read about two friends that dream the same dream. You'll see that a bear and a mouse can find something they both like. You'll see that people can be different but also alike.

Story characters can be your friends. You might find that you and they laugh or cry at the same things. There are many people and animals to meet. Turn the page and say hello.

Sincerely,
The Authors

CONTENTS

Theme: FRIENDS LIKE US / 92

BOOKSHELF

THE COW THAT WENT OINK

by Bernard Most

All the animals laugh when the cow goes OINK. This makes the cow sad. Then the cow meets a pig who goes MOO. This story tells what happens when the cow and the pig get together.

Award-Winning Author

Harcourt Brace Library Book

MY NEW BOY

by Joan Phillips

A little black puppy finds a boy of his own. The puppy teaches the boy all kinds of games and tricks. You will laugh at the funny things in this story.

Award-Winning Author

Harcourt Brace Library Book

SING A SONG OF PEOPLE

by Lois Lenski

Follow a boy and his dog as they walk through a busy city. You will meet many people along the way.

Award-Winning Author

ANIMAL MOTHERS

by Atsushi Komori

How did your mother care for you when you were a baby? <u>Animal Mothers</u> will show you the many ways animal babies are cared for.

DO LIKE KYLA

by Angela Johnson

Good things happen all day when sisters are also friends. A little sister learns a lot from her big sister, Kyla. But Kyla learns from her little sister, too.

Child Study Children's Book of the Year

THEME

Let's Get Together

Who are the people that are special to you?
Read about some friends and families.

CONTENTS

TOGETHER

by George Ella Lyon
Pictures by Vera Rosenberry

You cut the timber
and I'll build the house.

You bring the cheese
and I'll fetch the mouse.

You salt the ice
and I'll crank the cream.

Let's put our heads together

and dream the same dream.

I'll drive the truck
   if you'll fight the fire.

I'll plunk the keys
if you'll be the choir.

I'll find the ball
if you'll call the team.

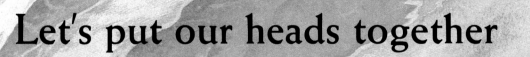

Let's put our heads together

and dream the same dream.

You dig for water
and I'll make a pail.

I'll paint the boat
if you'll set the sail.

You catch the fish
and I'll catch the stream!

Let's put our heads together

and dream the same dream.

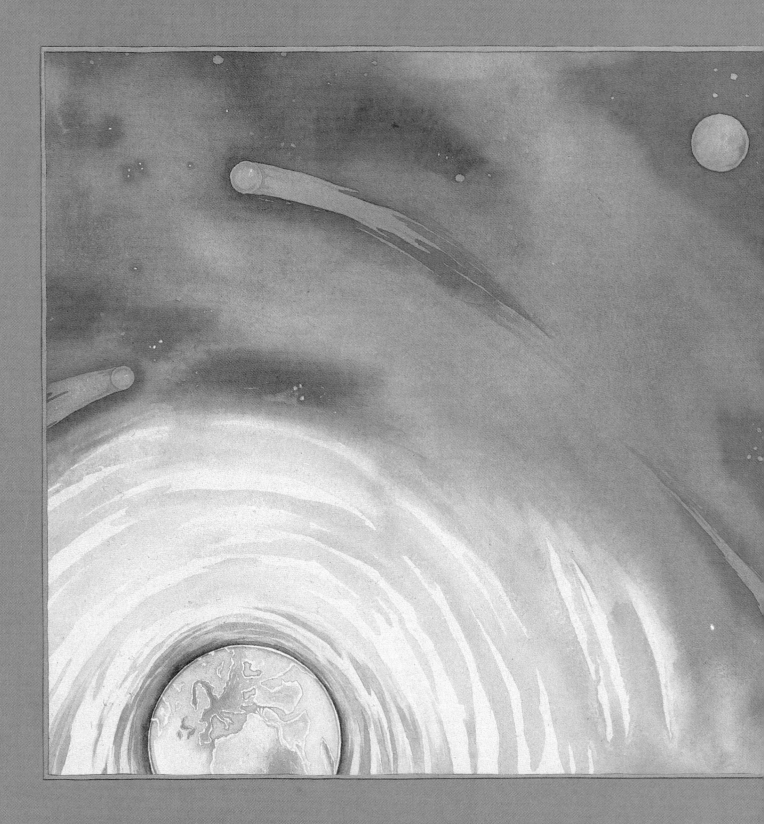

37

words and music by Ella Jenkins

illustrated by Jackie Snider

You'll sing a song, and I'll sing a song,
Then we'll sing a song together.
You'll sing a song, and I'll sing a song,
In warm or wintry weather.

You'll play a tune, and I'll play a tune,
Then we'll play a tune together.
You'll play a tune, and I'll play a tune,
In warm or wintry weather.

Five Little Monkeys
Jumping on the Bed

EILEEN CHRISTELOW

It was bedtime. So five little monkeys took a bath.

Five little monkeys put on their pajamas.

Five little monkeys brushed their teeth.

Five little monkeys said good night to their mama.

44

Then . . . five little monkeys jumped on the bed!

One fell off and bumped his head.

The mama called the doctor. The doctor said,

46

"No more monkeys jumping on the bed!"

So four little monkeys . . .

47

. . . jumped on the bed.

One fell off and bumped his head.

The mama called the doctor.

The doctor said,

"No more monkeys jumping on the bed!"

So three little monkeys jumped on the bed.

One fell off and bumped her head.

The mama called the doctor.

The doctor said,

"No more monkeys jumping on the bed!"

So two little monkeys jumped on the bed.

One fell off and bumped his head.

The mama called the doctor.

The doctor said,

"No more monkeys jumping on the bed!"

So one little monkey jumped on the bed.

She fell off and bumped her head.

The mama called the doctor.

The doctor said,

"NO MORE MONKEYS JUMPING ON THE BED!"

So five little monkeys fell fast asleep.

"Thank goodness!" said the mama.

"Now I can go to bed!"

Some Things Go Together

FROM
SOME THINGS GO TOGETHER

Peace with dove
Home with love
Gardens with flowers
Clocks with hours
Moths with screen
Grass with green
Leaves with tree
and you with me.

by Charlotte Zolotow

Garden in Bloom
Claude Monet
1840–1926

Whose Baby?

Masayuki Yabuuchi

Baby?

This is a fawn.
Whose baby is it?

A fawn is a baby deer.

It belongs to a father
and mother deer,
called a buck and a doe.

Whose chick is this?

It belongs to a peacock
and peahen.

74

75

This cub is curled up fast asleep.
Whose baby is it?

It is a fox cub.

It belongs to a fox and a vixen.

This cub is wide awake —
whose cub is it?

It belongs to a lion and lioness.

83

This is a pup —
whose pup is it?

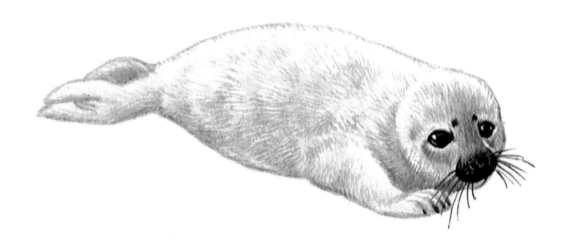

It belongs to a bull seal
and a cow seal.

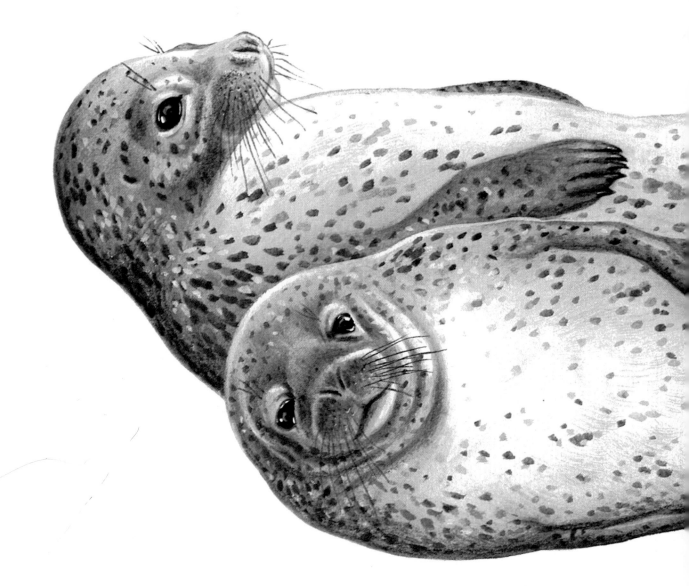

This is a calf.
Whose baby is it?

It is a baby bison.
It belongs to a bull bison
and a cow bison.

THEME

Friends Like Us

What does it take to be a friend?
Here are some stories about how
friendships work.

CONTENTS

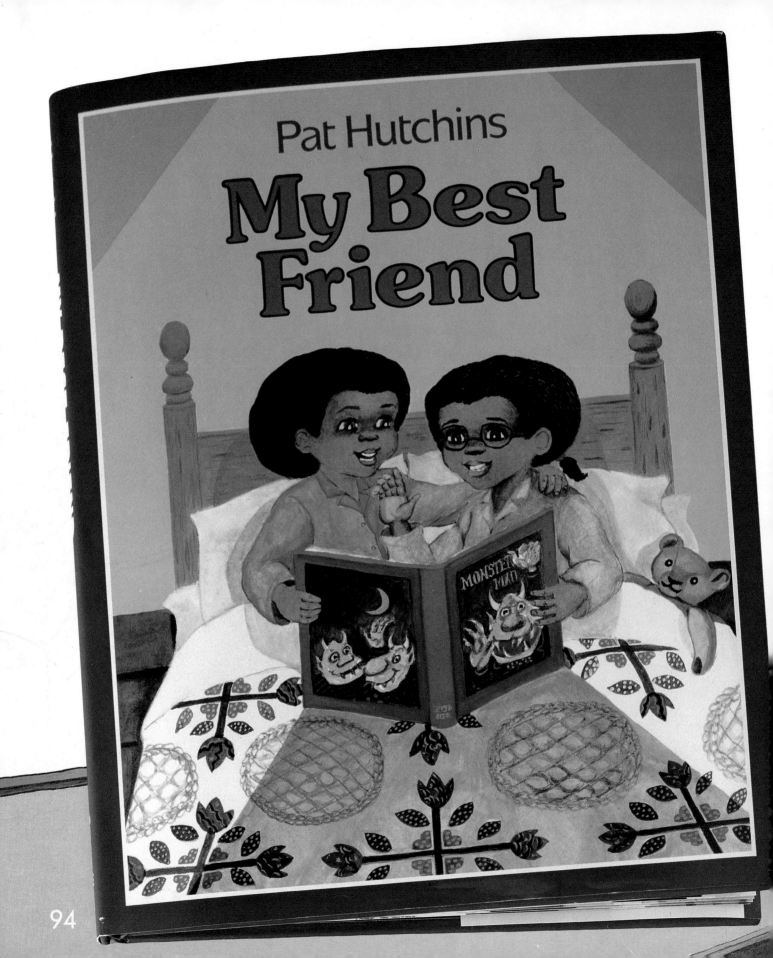

My best friend is coming
to spend the night.
I'm glad she's my best friend.

My best friend knows how to run faster

and climb higher

and jump farther than anyone.
I'm glad she's my best friend.

My best friend can eat spaghetti with a fork and doesn't drop any on the table.

My best friend knows how to
paint good pictures and doesn't
get fingermarks on the paper.

My best friend knows
how to untie her shoelaces

and how to do up the buttons on
her pajamas.

My best friend knows how to read. I'm glad she's my best friend.

My best friend thinks
there's a monster in the room.
But I know there isn't.

I know it's only the wind
blowing the curtains.

And I know if I close the window,
the curtains won't blow.

"I'm glad you're my best friend,"
said my best friend.

AWARD-WINNING
AUTHOR

HOW
JOE
THE BEAR
AND
SAM
THE MOUSE
GOT
TOGETHER

BEATRICE SCHENK DE REGNIERS

ILLUSTRATED BY
BERNICE MYERS

Call me Joe.

Call me Sam.

Hi, Sam.   Hi, Joe.

Where are you going,
Sam?

**Where are YOU going,
Joe?**

112

I am looking
for a place to live.

I am looking
for a place to live, too.
We can live together!

113

I like to live
in a BIG house.

I like to live
in a little house.

114

Then we cannot
live together.
Boo hoo.

Boo hoo.

We can play ball together!
I like to play football.

I like to
play baseball.

Then we cannot
play ball together.
Boo hoo!

Boo hoo!

Do you like
to ride a bike?

Yes.
I love to ride a bike.

We can ride a bike together!
I like to ride slow.

I like to ride fast.

Then we cannot
ride a bike together.

Boo hoo.

Boo hoo.

We can play music together!
I like violin music.

I like drum music.

I hate violin music.

Then we cannot
play music
together.

Boo hoo.
Good-bye, Sam.

Boo hoo.
Good-bye,
Joe.

126

Where are you going,
Sam?

Where are YOU going,
Joe?

127

It is three o'clock.
I am going to get ice cream.
Every day at three o'clock
I eat ice cream.

I am going to get ice cream, too.
Every day at three o'clock
I eat ice cream.

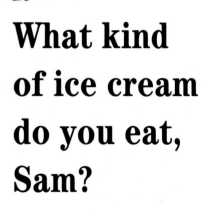

**What kind
of ice cream
do you eat,
Sam?**

All kinds of ice cream.

131

I eat all kinds of ice cream, too.

Then we can eat ice cream together!

You will live in a big house.
I will live in a little house.

You will play football and ride slow.
I will play baseball and ride fast.

You will play violin music.
I will play drum music.

But every day
at three o'clock . . .

Yes. Every day
at three o'clock . . .

FRiEND

When
he wills
his quills
to stand on
end

I'm very glad
that
I'm a friend

of
Porcupine.

by Lilian Moore
illustrated by Diane Borowski

MOUSE TALES

VERY TALL MOUSE AND VERY SHORT MOUSE

BY ARNOLD LOBEL

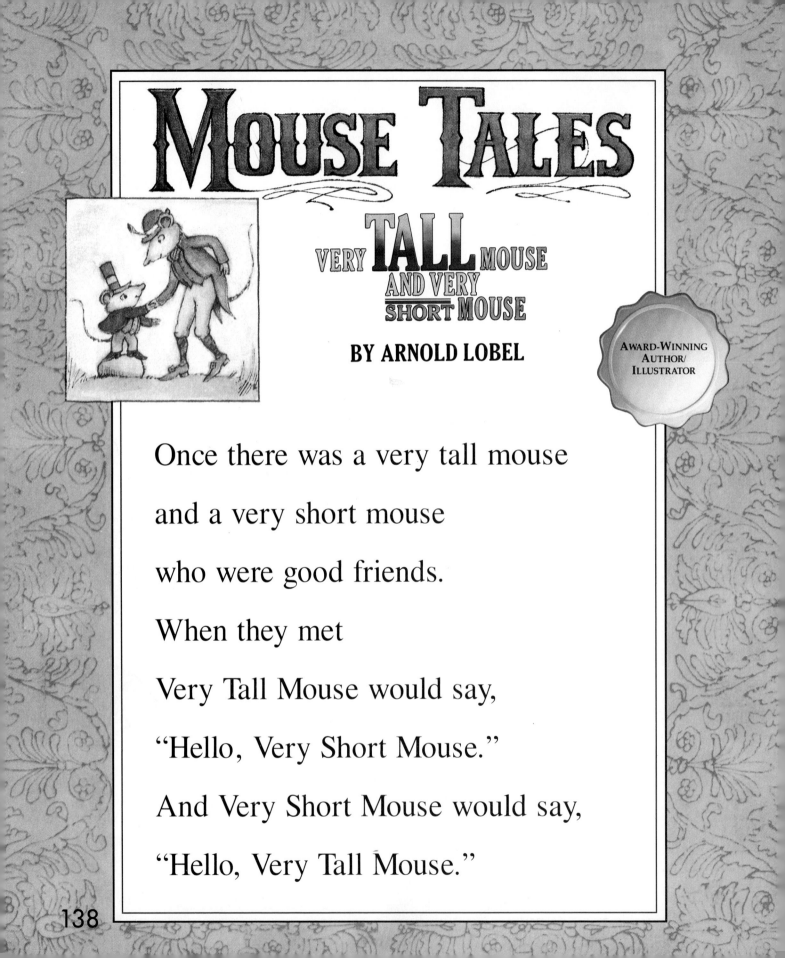

Once there was a very tall mouse

and a very short mouse

who were good friends.

When they met

Very Tall Mouse would say,

"Hello, Very Short Mouse."

And Very Short Mouse would say,

"Hello, Very Tall Mouse."

The two friends would often

take walks together.

As they walked along

Very Tall Mouse would say,

"Hello birds."

And Very Short Mouse would say,

"Hello bugs."

When they passed

by a garden

Very Tall Mouse would say,

"Hello flowers."

And Very Short Mouse

would say,

"Hello roots."

When they passed by a house

Very Tall Mouse would say,

"Hello roof."

And Very Short Mouse

would say,

"Hello cellar."

One day the two mice

were caught in a storm.

Very Tall Mouse said,

"Hello raindrops."

And Very Short Mouse said,

"Hello puddles."

They ran indoors to get dry.

"Hello ceiling,"

said Very Tall Mouse.

"Hello floor,"

said Very Short Mouse.

Soon the storm was over.

The two friends

ran to the window.

Very Tall Mouse held

Very Short Mouse up to see.

"Hello rainbow!"

they both said together.